SUN AND RAIN

Exploring Seasons in Hawai'i

Stephanie Feeney

A Latitude 20 Book
University of Hawai'i Press
Honolulu

ISBN: 978-0-8248-3088-5

University of Hawai'i Press books
are printed on acid-free paper and
meet the guidelines for permanence
and durability of the Council on
Library Resources.

Designed by Barbara Pope Book Design

Printed by C & C Offset Printing Co., Ltd.

ABOUT THIS BOOK

Every year, everyplace, there are changes in the weather that are called seasons. In Hawai'i we can best describe a year as having two seasons—the dry time of year, from May through October, and the wet time of year, from November through April. The dry season is usually sunny and warm, and there is not very much rain. The wet season is cooler, there is more rain, and the weather often changes.

The seasons in Hawai'i influence people's activities, the way plants grow, and how animals behave. Hawai'i's seasons are not as easy to see as the seasons in many other parts of the world, but you can find clues to tell you what the season is and when it is going to change. The signs are not as obvious as snow falling or green leaves changing to gold and red, but if you pay attention, you can see and feel the seasonal changes.

Knowing about Hawai'i's seasons can help people who live on the islands to understand and appreciate changes that occur every year. Information about Hawai'i's seasons lets people who live in other places learn that not everyone has seasons just like their own. In schools everywhere, children learn about the four seasons—winter, spring, summer, and fall—that occur in cooler climates. Even in Hawai'i, though, students may not learn about the two seasons that they experience at home.

Sun and Rain will show you some of the signs you can look for that tell you what the season is in Hawai'i. It also provides information about why there are seasons everywhere and why the seasons in Hawai'i are different than those in many other places.

In Hawai‘i it is almost always warm and
sunny during the dry season.
Strong, steady trade winds blow most of the time.
Children play in the surf and sand.

In the wet season, some days are cool (but never very cold), some are rainy, and others are sunny and warm. Nights can be cool, so it's nice to curl up with a book and a cozy blanket.

In the dry, sunny season, children wear bathing suits and light clothing.

In the wet, rainy season, children sometimes wear long pants and jackets. And they may need an umbrella on a rainy day. Except at the tops of the mountains, no one needs a warm coat or gloves.

In the dry, sunny season, children like
to eat cool treats like shave ice.

In the wet, rainy season, they enjoy
hot foods like soup with noodles.

You can tell it's the dry season when the ocean on the north shores of the islands is flat or the waves are small.

People swim, kayak, and snorkel in the calm water.

You can tell it's the wet season when you see surfers riding big waves on the north shores of the islands.

There are many kinds of colorful flowering trees
in Hawai'i. Gold trees bloom in the wet season.
By the time the dry season comes, jacarandas,
poincianas, and shower trees are covered
with beautiful flowers.

In the wet, rainy season, the hills turn green.

You can see
rushing streams
and hear roaring
waterfalls.

In the wet season, there can be storms
and lots of wind and rain.
Clouds move down the mountains
carrying rain showers.

On the island of Hawai'i, snow covers
the peaks of the volcano called Mauna Kea.
Sometimes there is enough snow to go skiing.

One way to tell the season is to look
at plumeria trees. In the rainy season,
the trees lose their leaves. Later, flowers
begin to bloom on the branches.

In the dry season, the branches are covered
with leaves and fragrant flowers.

Mango trees flower in the rainy season.
Some of the flowers slowly turn into fruit.

When the dry season arrives, the fruit ripens
and you can eat delicious mangoes.

In the rainy season, humpback whales
swim back to Hawai'i from Alaska, where they have
been feeding on tiny shrimp in the icy waters.
They give birth to their babies
in Hawai'i's warm ocean.

Kōlea, Pacific golden plovers, can be seen
on grassy fields during the rainy season.
Toward the end of the season,
most of their feathers begin to get darker.
That means they are getting ready
to fly to Alaska, where they will
lay their eggs and hatch their chicks.

In the dry season, *honu*, green sea turtles,
lay eggs in nests on the beaches.
The eggs lie hidden in the sand for two months.
Before the rainy season comes, they hatch
and the baby turtles make their way
to the ocean where they will live.

You can also see signs of the seasons
in Hawai'i by looking at the sky at night.
In the warm months of the dry season,
look for the constellation Scorpio, the scorpion.

During the wet season,
you can see the constellation Orion,
the hunter, in the night sky.

In the dry season, people in Hawaiʻi
celebrate American Independence Day
on the Fourth of July with fireworks.

Christmas comes during the rainy season.
Children open presents under the Christmas tree,
and you might see a decorated tree at the beach.
But, except on the highest mountains, there is
no snow, so there is never a white Christmas.

On warm summer evenings,
Bon Dances are held at Japanese temples.
People dressed in traditional clothing dance
around a tower decorated with paper lanterns
to the steady rhythm of the *taiko* drums.

The new year begins in the rainy season.
Many people in Hawaiʻi celebrate the
Chinese New Year.

You can hear firecrackers
and see a colorful Lion Dance.
Feeding money to the lion is
supposed to bring good luck.

And all children, everywhere, have their very own special day—their birthday. It is often celebrated with a party and a birthday cake. Is your birthday in the rainy season or the dry season?

Look for the signs of the seasons.
Listen to the wind.
Feel the air on your face.
Watch the sun and clouds in the
daytime and the sky at night.
Pay careful attention to the plants,
animals, and activities you see around you.
You will discover the seasons in Hawai'i!

NOVEMBER

DECEMBER

JANUARY

FEBRUARY

MARCH

APRIL

MAY

JUNE

JULY

AUGUST

SEPTEMBER

OCTOBER

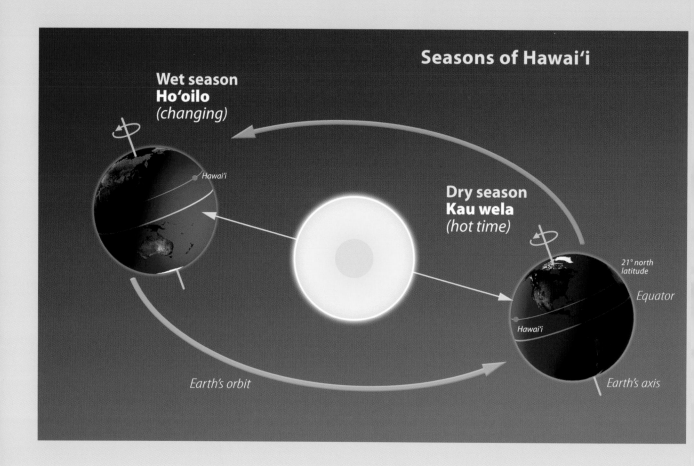

ABOUT SEASONS

The following sections are written for teachers, family members, and older children. The information can be discussed with younger children if they are interested in learning more.

Why are there seasons? The Earth gets all of its heat and light from the sun, so whether we see darkness or light and feel warm or cold depends on how the light of the sun falls on the Earth.

The Earth moves in an enormous circle called an *orbit* (imagine walking all around the outside of a big building). A year is defined as the time it takes for the Earth to move in its orbit all the way around the sun. You can tell the Earth is moving around the sun when you look at the star patterns at night. As the Earth moves, different groups of stars become visible at different times of the year.

The Earth also *rotates* once a day (like a spinning top). In fact, the word "day" refers to the time it takes for one rotation. When the side of the Earth that we are on is facing the sun, it is daytime for us. As the Earth rotates, we begin to face away from the sun, and it becomes night.

The Earth has an *axis* (an imaginary straight line) about which it rotates. The poles of the Earth (the northern and southern tips of the axis) stay pointed in the same direction all the time. But the axis is not perpendicular (straight up and down) with regard to the plane of the Earth's orbit. It is tilted as shown in the diagram on the opposite page. So part of the year, as the Earth revolves around the sun, the northern hemisphere is tilted toward the sun, and part of the year the southern hemisphere is tilted toward the sun. The part of the Earth that tilts toward the sun is warmer, while the part that tilts away is colder.

In June the part of the Earth where Hawai'i is located faces directly toward the sun. At that time of year, the sun is nearly overhead during midday so the islands get a lot of sunlight and it is very warm.

But in December the islands of Hawai'i are tilted away from the sun. Because the sunlight falls at an angle, we don't get as much sunlight as in June, so it is cooler.

The seasons are also influenced by the distance between a particular place on the Earth and the *equator* (an imaginary line that goes around the middle of the Earth, halfway between the poles). Weather in places nearer to the equator does not change as much as it does in places that are closer to the north and south poles. Because Hawai'i is fairly close to the equator, changes in sunlight between summer and winter are not very great, and the temperature doesn't change very much throughout the year. Farther from the equator, the surface of the Earth is always tilted away from the sun, but less so in the summer, so it is warmer than it is in the winter. In places far north or south of the equator, the weather varies greatly between summer and winter.

The tilt of the Earth also affects the length of the day. During the warm times of year, the days are longer, and in the cooler times of year, they are shorter.

ABOUT SEASONS IN HAWAI'I

The people who lived in Hawai'i a long time ago described the year as having two seasons. They called the dry, sunny season, when the sun is overhead and the trade winds are blowing, *kau* or *kau wela* (which means the hot time of year). They called the wet, cooler season, when the sun is lower and the winds more variable, *ho'oilo* (which means changing).

The ancient Hawaiians needed to pay attention to the seasons so they would know when to plant their crops, when to look for food plants and animals, and when it was safe to take their canoes out fishing. Changes in the seasons are not as important today because most people buy their food in stores and travel in cars and airplanes. People in Hawai'i today who fish and farm the land still pay careful attention to changes in the season. And the way the ancient Hawaiians looked at the seasons helps everyone to understand the changes that we experience every year.

Lo'i kalo: a taro paddy

Most of the time during the dry season, gentle winds called trade winds blow from the northeast, so we call the shores of the islands that face northeast the *windward* side (from the sailing term that means the direction from which the wind is blowing). The air picks up moisture as it moves across the ocean and clouds form. As the clouds pass over the island mountaintops, they cool and may produce showers. The mountains shield the western side of each of the islands (called *leeward* from another sailing term) from the trade wind showers, so it is warmer and dryer there.

The ocean gets a little warmer during the dry season. The extra heat contributes to the formation of hurricanes over the ocean. These storms may bring wind and rain close to the shores of the islands. Sometimes one passes directly over the islands, causing huge waves and fierce winds that knock down trees and buildings.

During the wet season, other storms form over the ocean. These storms, pushed by the wind, pass to the north of Hawai'i. As they pass, winds from the southwest (called Kona winds) replace the normal northeast trade winds and bring dark clouds and heavy rain. The storms cause big waves on the north shores of the islands.

The temperature of the ocean doesn't change very much throughout the year. In the summer, the ocean keeps the air from getting too hot, so Hawai'i's summers are mild compared to places that get the same amount of sun but are farther from the ocean. In the wet season, the ocean keeps the air from becoming very cold, so our winters are not as cool as they are in other parts of the world.

The temperature in Hawai'i also varies with the height, or *elevation*, of the land between the shoreline and the mountains. It is warmest near the ocean, the lowest place in the islands, and coolest at the tops of the mountains. On top of the very tallest mountains, it sometimes snows. If you live in Hawai'i, you know that differences in elevation can influence the weather as much as the seasons do.

SHARING THIS BOOK WITH CHILDREN

How you share *Sun and Rain* with children will depend on the ages of the children and whether you are a caring adult or a teacher.

Younger children will be most interested in the photographs. Read the book aloud and talk to them about what they see. Encourage them to remember their experiences by asking questions like, "When do the trees near our house/school have flowers?" and "When do you use your umbrella?" and "What is the weather like at Christmas where you live?" During the year you can also help them become aware of seasonal changes around them. Help them to observe things like a tree in the neighborhood that begins to flower, rainfall and wind patterns, and grass turning dry and brown and then green again.

Older children are ready to learn more about the science of the seasons. You can share the information in the previous sections of this book with them. To illustrate the impact of the angle of the sun, you can give a child a piece of cardboard that is black on one side and white on the other. Have the child hold it so that the black side is directly facing the sun. Ask the child to touch the back of the board and notice how warm it feels. Then have the child turn the cardboard so that it is at an angle to the sun and, after a while, feel the difference in temperature on the board. Ask why she or he thinks it was different. This activity will help children to understand that the angle of the sun's rays changes the temperature of the cardboard as it absorbs more or less sunlight.

As you study the seasons in Hawai'i, you can help children to become more aware of changes in the weather and length of day at different times of year, and to notice things people do when the weather changes. You can also show them a globe, look at Hawai'i's location, and discuss how living on an island near the equator influences how people live and what they do. You could have them look at the locations of other places that they are familiar with and talk about how the weather in those places might be similar to or different from that in Hawai'i, and how it might influence the lives of the people who live there.

Hukilau: to fish together by pulling one big net

Most children are interested in animals and will enjoy learning more about the animals discussed in this book. If possible, provide them with direct experience of the animals at the aquarium, the zoo, the beach, or in your neighborhood. When direct experience is not possible, there are good children's books available about the *kōlea*, the humpback whale, and the *honu*.

You can also read books to children and talk to them about changes in animals' behavior at different times of the year. If you are a teacher, you may want to have the children in your class study the animals discussed in this book, animals in other places that make seasonal migrations, or animals whose appearance or activities change with the season.

Acknowledgments

I want to express my thanks and profound appreciation to all of the people who helped me to turn the idea of a book about the seasons in Hawai'i into a reality:

My husband, Dr. Donald Mickey, for his interest and support, expertise in astronomy, and commitment to making knowledge of science accessible to young children. His participation in writing about the effects of the movement of the solar system on the seasons is an essential part of this book.

My friend and colleague Eva Moravcik for her insights into appropriate content for young children and for her skill in word crafting.

Lilinoe Andrews for recognizing the value of a book about seasons for children in Hawai'i and for sharing research on how ancient Hawaiians regarded the seasons.

Jane Dickson Iijima for friendship, encouragement, commitment to a meaningful science curriculum for young children, and helpful comments on the manuscript.

Rheta Kuwahara for her enthusiasm for this project and for setting up photo sessions.

Hugh Mosher, Susan Boynton, and Sharon Dahlquist for assistance with photography; Dr. Jeff Kuhn and Dr. Richard Criley for scientific consultation; and Native Books/Nā Mea Hawai'i for the loan of a Hawaiian quilt.

Karen Teramura, at the University of Hawai'i Institute for Astronomy, for designing the graphic of the solar system.

My students in early childhood education at University of Hawai'i at Mānoa and the many teachers of young children who shared their ideas and assured me that there was a need for a book about the seasons in Hawai'i.

The wonderful children of Hawai'i whose pictures grace these pages, and the families who participated in photo sessions and allowed us to use photographs of their children in this book.

Masako Ikeda, editor at University of Hawai'i Press, who has supported my efforts and championed this book from the beginning.

And finally, to Shelley Yorita for a discussion under a jacaranda tree on the island of Maui that was the inspiration for this book.

Photography Credits

Photographs on the pages listed below were taken by the following:

David and Sue Boynton: i, 8, 9, 13 (poinciana, shower tree), 15, 20, 21, 23, 40, 41, 42

Ron Dahlquist: iv–v, vi, 4, 10–11, 13 (jacaranda), 17, 22, 25, 29

Moku Kaaloa: 30, 31

Melissa Kim Mosher: front cover, ii, 2, 6, 7

Jeff Reese: 5, 13 (gold tree), 16, 18, 19, 32, 33, 34, 35

Additional photographs were taken by Barbara Pope (pp. 12, 14), Mary Van de Ven (p. 28), and Jim Watt (p. 24 and back cover).

Note for orientation: Page 2 shows a boy reading a book with his mother.

About the Author

Dr. Stephanie Feeney is Professor of Education Emerita at the University of Hawai'i at Mānoa. She is the author of three other children's books about Hawai'i published by University of Hawai'i Press: *A is for Aloha*, *Hawai'i is a Rainbow*, and *Sand to Sea*. She has also written extensively about the field of early childhood education.

About the Photographers

The great majority of the images in this book are the work of five talented photographers: Jeff Reese, Moku Kaaloa, and Melissa Kim Mosher (the island of O'ahu), Ron Dahlquist (the island of Maui), and the late David Boynton (the island of Kaua'i).